SO WHAT!

LEARNING ABOUT BAD ATTITUDES

Katherine Eason

FOX EYE
PUBLISHING

Rhys sometimes had a **BAD ATTITUDE**.
He didn't do what he was told.
Sometimes, he was rude and cheeky.

Mrs Spud was upset with Rhys and Rhia. But Rhys **DIDN'T CARE**. He stuck out his tongue!

Rhia and Rhys hid behind the hedge. He shouted **RUDE WORDS** at Mrs Spud. Rhys thought it was funny.

Mrs Spud was **CROSS**.
She told Mum what had happened.

Mum told Rhys she didn't like **RUDE WORDS**. She told Rhys to say sorry to Mrs Spud.

Rhys said he wouldn't say sorry.
He said Mum couldn't make him.
Then, he **STOMPED OFF**.

Mum told Rhys he couldn't have his ball if he didn't say sorry. She told him to put the ball away. But Rhys kicked the ball across the room.

After dinner, Mum asked Rhys to dry the dishes. Rhys said no way. He said he didn't want to.

Mum said she liked it better when Rhys **SPOKE NICELY** to her. She liked it better when Rhys had a **GOOD ATTITUDE**.

Later, Mum gave Rhys a hug. Then, she asked him how he would feel if someone said rude or unkind words to him. What if someone spoilt his vegetables or stuck their tongue out at him?

Rhys thought about how that might feel. It **WOULDN'T FEEL GOOD**. Maybe having a good attitude was important.

The next day, Rhys said sorry to Mrs Spud and helped her to plant some more vegetables. He helped Mum dry the dishes after lunch, too.

Mum smiled at Rhys, and he smiled back. Having a **GOOD ATTITUDE FELT GOOD**.

Words and Behaviour

Rhys had a bad attitude in this story and that caused a lot of problems.

BAD ATTITUDE

DIDN'T CARE

There are a lot of words to do with having a bad attitude in this book. Can you remember all of them?

RUDE WORDS

STOMPED OFF

Let's talk about feelings and manners

This series helps children to understand difficult emotions and behaviours and how to manage them. The characters in the series have been created to show emotions and behaviours that are often seen in young children, and which can be difficult to manage.

So What!

The story in this book examines the reasons for having a bad attitude. It looks at why having a good attitude is important and stops others from becoming upset.

How to use this book

You can read this book with one child or a group of children. The book can be used to begin a discussion around complex behaviour such as having a bad attitude.

 The book is also a reading aid, with enlarged and repeated words to help children to develop their reading skills.

How to read the story

Before beginning the story, ensure that the children you are reading to are relaxed and focused.

Take time to look at the enlarged words and the illustrations, and discuss what this book might be about before reading the story.

New words can be tricky for young children to approach. Sounding them out first, slowly and repeatedly, can help children to learn the words and become familiar with them.

How to discuss the story

When you have finished reading the story, use these questions and discussion points to examine the theme of the story with children and explore the emotions and behaviour within it:
- What do you think the story was about?
- Have you been in a situation in which you showed a bad attitude? What was that situation?
- Do you think having a bad attitude doesn't matter? Why?
- Do you think having a good attitude is important? Why?
- What could go wrong if you have a bad attitude?

Titles in the series

   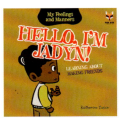 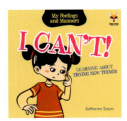

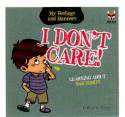 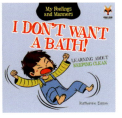   

   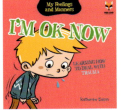 

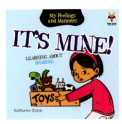   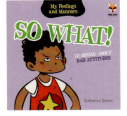 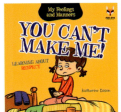

First published in 2023 by Fox Eye Publishing
Unit 31, Vulcan House Business Centre,
Vulcan Road, Leicester, LE5 3EF
www.foxeyepublishing.com

Copyright © 2023 Fox Eye Publishing
All rights reserved. No portion of this book may be reproduced in any form without permission from the publisher, except as permitted by U.K. copyright law.

Author: Katherine Eason
Art director: Paul Phillips
Cover designer: Emma Bailey
Editor: Jenny Rush

All illustrations by Novel

ISBN 978-1-80445-161-8

Printed in China